Black Beyond the Myths
WOMAN WORKING

J. Kelly, Ph.D.

Black Woman Working: Beyond the Myths

J. Kelly, Ph.D.

Published by

J. Kelly

United States of America

ISBN: 978-0-692-05228-0

Cover Design: Walter 'DI' Stevenson (Main Contributor)
Cover Art: Veronica Ariel

DEDICATION

To my daughters, with love.

CONTENTS

Acknowledgments

ACKNOWLEDGMENTS

I would like to thank my entire extended family for loving who I am and the work that I have done for as long as I can remember. To my mother, aunts, sisters, and sister-cousins who allowed me to vent, who shared in my whirlwinds of emotions, and always made sure I knew I was lovable, worthy, and intelligent. This could not have been written without your emotional support. I would like to thank my soulmate, for not being afraid of this book, for encouraging me to continue writing when I didn't know where to turn, and for always acting in love. Your partnership is everything. To the readers who allowed me to share my early drafts, I am forever grateful for your insight and encouragement. I also would like to thank everyone in my life who have talked with me about the issues described in this book. There are too many beautiful people to name, but, you know who you are. Thank you for sharing in the moments and for the dialogue. To my editor, graphic designers, and artist thank you for your vision, patience, and contributions to this book. We did it! Lastly, I would like to thank my foremothers for their sacrifices and the Black feminist scholars who are currently in the trenches working day in and day out for liberation. I am inspired, and I thank you.

1

INTRODUCTION

"Moving from silence into speech is for the oppressed, the colonized, the exploited, and those who stand in struggle side by side a gesture of defiance that heals, that makes new life and new growth possible. It is that act of speech, of 'talking back,' that is no mere gesture of empty words, that is the experience of our movement from object to subject—the liberated voice."

~bell hooks, *Talking Back: Thinking Feminist, Thinking Black*, 1989, p. 9

I value justice, balance, and a life lived with purpose. Two years ago, I left a full-time job, for the second time, and exited the paid labor market because these values were threatened as I attempted to navigate the world as a Black Woman Worker. The act of leaving was traumatic; I had defied the mythical image of the modern-day Black (Super)

Woman who is career-oriented, financially independent, and emotionally unbreakable. But amid this trauma, I've reimagined myself, achieved a new level of consciousness, and found some quiet after the storm. During my quiet reflection, I began to write—with a *liberated voice*. This is my story. Black. Woman. Working.

Who Am I?

There are a few things about myself that I would like to disclose at the start. I am a 37-year-old African-American woman. I am happily married, and I have two young children. Growing up, I had an awesome mother who did the very best she could to care for her six children, with the help of a supportive extended family. I take mothering seriously because I want to be for my children what my mother and extended family were for me—unwavering sources of love, guidance, and protection. I also want to be all that they were not able to be for various reasons.

I am on the cusp of Generation X and Y. Generational divisions are not just clichés; they represent cohorts coming of age in the context of significant demographic, historical, social, economic, and/or political shifts that influence a group of people's behaviors, values, and attitudes. Although boundaries vary, Generation Xers were born between 1965 and 1980. This generation is sandwiched between the larger cohorts of Baby

Boomers, born between 1946 and 1964, and Millennials, who were born after 1980 (Pew Research Center, 2015). My worldviews have been influenced by growing up during a time of high work demands being placed on families, recessions, and the influx of highly addictive drugs into poor communities, which all required children to take care of themselves (latchkey) at an earlier age than the previous generation. We also witnessed failures in the social, political, and economic systems along with the paranoia of Y2K. Because of being born in this time, I value my independence, I have a healthy skepticism of institutions, and I work to live not live to work because the world could end tomorrow. In a world that seems quite chaotic, I strive for balance in all areas of my life. Being good at my job and enjoying a high quality of life are equally important. Being on the cusp of the millennial generation, I also see myself as a change agent. I am motivated by the belief that I have a responsibility to make the world better and improve my communities. So, I need space for that, too.

I have a doctorate in the field of Human Development and Family Studies. Over the years, I've been inundated with information, statistics, theory, and research on what helps and hinders child development and family systems, first as a graduate student, then as a family life and human development specialist, and also while on the faculty of a human development and family studies program. As such, I must admit, I am vigilant when it comes to caring for my own children, family, and community—I find myself constantly watching out for potential threats and opportunities. To further complicate things, my sociological imagination is constantly uncovering structural inequalities. So, I am constantly resisting oppression with all my might; oppression feels like no matter what door you walk through, pain is on the other side waiting to swallow you whole.

Why Am I Writing This?

Initially when I was asked why I left my jobs, I would go silent. My body would just become flooded with memories and emotions, and I would be unable to retrieve words to express my feelings. Some months after I left my second full-time position as an assistant professor, I realized I needed to collect my thoughts on leaving. I started writing this story to answer the 'why' question for myself and others who wanted an explanation for my abrupt departure from paid, full-time employment. As I began to write about my experiences, writing became less about answering the question of why I left and more about sharing my story in an intellectual way.

In sharing my story using a Black feminist epistemology, I am engaging in a social justice project that involves naming forms of oppression and identifying ways that society can reorganize to counteract them. This work is inherently political. I take a stand on issues that I found important as an African-American married woman with children, and a worker; and in doing so, I created space to advocate for change. So, you see, I have become an activist of sorts and I am writing my story to help catalyze Black women workers into action in ways they find empowering. These actions include: staying, leaving, advocating, pondering, discussing, and organizing. I am hopeful that what I write will help others. Even if it only helps one person improve their work experiences, having undertaken this writing project will be worthwhile.

I hope that readers will not see this work as an effort to expose any one person or institution (I do not reference people or institutions by name in this book); I am only interested in uncovering structural issues that are common across individuals and work spaces. I am not writing this to complain, blame, or otherwise compensate for an inability to handle "a hard job." I could have told that story in private. However, I took a risk in making my private experiences public. I am totally exposed; and I hope that by coming to know my experiences, readers will better understand their own experiences. I hope they will see themselves or someone they know in these pages, gain a deeper understanding of Black women workers, and perhaps decide to advocate for themselves and others in the workplace and at home. I hope it helps people.

What Does that Even Mean?

Before getting into my experiences as a Black woman worker, let us spend some time with the general ideas at play and give attention to a few of the important terms that I reference in telling my story. C. Wright Mills coined the term sociological imagination in 1959 to describe a state of mind that allows an individual to recognize the interconnections between historical and contemporary features of society and people's everyday lives. Mills (2000) wrote, "To be aware of the idea of social structure and to use it with sensibility is to be capable of tracing such linkages among a wide variety of milieu. To be able to do that is to possess the sociological imagination" (p. 11). So, when I mentioned my sociological imagination, I was referring to my ability to situate my private troubles within socio-cultural and historical contexts and identify the public issues underlying them. I use my sociological imagination to tell parts of my story.

Black feminist thought informs my sociological imagination and my thinking about how society influences people's everyday lives. "Rather than being a White-identified anomaly within U.S. Black community development efforts, Black feminism can better be seen as an intercontinental Black women's consciousness movement that addresses the concerns of women of African descent" (Collins, 2008, p. 252). In this story, I draw upon Black feminism to understand the ways race, class, and gender intersect in a matrix of domination. A matrix of domination "describes the overall social organization within which intersecting oppressions originate, develop, and are contained" (Collins, 2008, p. 246). I name the ways oppression operates and impacts the Black Woman Worker. To add, Black women's ideas and intellectual work has been suppressed in U.S. society. This work attempts to counter that suppression by reclaiming Black women's subjugated knowledges. In telling my story, I draw heavily upon the work of Black women intellectuals to analyze and interpret my private experiences in relation to public life.

Over the course of writing my story, exploitation was a recurrent theme. However, race, class, gender, and sexuality as systems within U.S. social structure intersect in ways that can also lead to activism (Collins, 2008). Black feminist thought is a vehicle for my resistance. I problematize the intersecting oppressions I encountered in everyday, work-related situations and rearticulate the act of leaving the labor market and laboring at home from a Black feminist standpoint. While interrogating my own work experiences, I engaged in what Patricia Hill Collins (2008) refers to as "part of a wider struggle for human dignity, empowerment and social justice" (p. 46). I intend for this project to bring Black women's paid and unpaid labor to the forefront of American consciousness and spark a shift in how women experience work in this country; Black feminist thought provides space for this sort of activism in intellectual work.

The term oppression is used throughout this story. I draw upon Marilyn Frye's (1983) conceptualization of the term that involves being pressed or "caught between or among forces" that work together to restrict, mold, flatten, or "immobilize." While reflecting upon my work experiences, Frye's double bind construct stood out the most. I found myself returning to this concept time and time again while writing my story. According to Frye, "One of the most ubiquitous features of the world as experienced by oppressed people is the double bind— situations in which options are reduced to very few, and all of them expose one to penalty, censure, or deprivation" (p. 11). Barriers and discomfort with situations at various moments in life are not the same as experiencing oppression. Frye distinguishes oppression from such experiences. She says oppression is like a birdcage and:

It is only when you step back, stop looking at the wires one by one, microscopically, and take a macroscopic view of the whole cage, that you can see why the bird does not go anywhere; and then you will see it in a moment that the bird is surrounded by a network of systematically related barriers (p. 12).

This birdcage analogy best describes what I refer to as oppression throughout the telling of my story.

Racism, sexism, and microaggression are other terms used throughout the recounting of my story—all are forms of oppression. My thoughts about racism are aligned with DeGruy's (2005) conceptualization of it as "the belief that people differ along biological and genetic lines and that one's own group is superior to another group. This belief is coupled with the power to negatively affect the lives of those perceived to be inferior" (p. 23). To be clear, my focus upon power is at the societal or group level and goes beyond what individuals accomplish or achieve. Sexism is "the belief in the inherent superiority of one sex and thereby the right to dominate" (Lorde, 1984, 2007, p. 45). Harris and Gonzalez (2012) succinctly conceptualizes microaggression as "subtle or blatant attempts at punishing the unexpected behavior" (p. 3). Microaggressions are the everyday, taken-for-granted ways that stereotypes operate in society, consciously and subconsciously.

Finally, I use Patricia Hill Collins' concept of motherwork throughout the book. Motherwork describes the reproductive labor that I perform for my family and community. It includes tasks such as bearing and caring for children, cooking, cleaning, (Duffy, 2007) managing relationships, planning, organizing, and a host of other activities.

How Did I Do This?

I conducted an autoethnography, which means I studied my own experiences within the context of larger social and cultural issues to be both reflexive and provocative. In the preface of her book "Creating Autoethnographies", Tessa Muncey (2010) says, "Who am I, must be the ultimate autoethnographic question" (p. xvi). I spent several months reflecting on this question and recording my thoughts and feelings of leaving my jobs and doing motherwork. I started to record my thoughts in a journal in the summer of 2016. After I stopped coming up with new thoughts, experiences, and notions to record in my journal, I began reading my entries and combining ideas that were similar. Eventually, I summarized combinations of ideas, thoughts, and notes to myself into a typed response to the "why did you leave" question. I also reflected on documents, emails, and student evaluations. Through these processes of reflection, I identified one major reason why I left; I was not happy with my work situations because I was experiencing various forms of oppression. I also pinpointed four ways my oppression was felt and organized my story around being a Black woman working.

This is intellectual work. As such, I interpreted my experiences within a larger socio-historical context using several different theoretical lenses. I used my sociological imagination grounded in Black feminist thought to interpret my experiences with race, gender, and worker oppression. I want this work to be accessible to and considered credible by African-American women workers and I hope that it is. As I interpreted and revised my writing, I simultaneously evaluated whether I was upholding standards for Black feminist intellectuals to be "personal advocates for their material, be accountable for the consequences of their work, have lived or experienced their material in some fashion, and be willing to engage in dialogue about their findings with ordinary, everyday people" (Collins, 2008, p. 285).

The following is a collection of my thoughts on being a Black Woman Worker. My thoughts have taken the shape of four individual essays, with a holistic quality and interconnections that beg to be considered in concert. Chapter two describes my experiences being Black in the academy and leaving my position as an assistant professor. In this chapter, I uncover hidden consequences of being a Black woman working in academia. Chapter three chronicles my experiences navigating a nine-to-five position as a married woman with children. This chapter names roadblocks associated with integrating work and parenting young children as a married, female, family life and human development specialist. Chapter four describes being a worker in both of my full-time professional positions and leaving them. In this chapter, I challenge notions of the ideal worker who is always present and overworked. In chapter five, I interrogate my recent experiences with unpaid, full-time motherwork. I reflect upon my current experiences working for free, and at home most of the time. In chapter six, I offer concluding thoughts, future directions, and recommendations for change.

2

BEING A BLACK WOMAN IN ACADEMIA

"Racism runs like poison through the blood of American society since Europeans first landed on these shores. And, since that beginning, America and Americans have invested much in denying it. America's and Americans' denial of their blatant racism and attending atrocities committed through the nation's history has become pathological. Such denial has allowed this illness to fester for almost 400 years. It keeps this country sick with this issue of race."

~Joy DeGruy, *Posttraumatic Slave Disorder: America's Legacy of Enduring Injury and Healing*, 2005, p. 20

I had never experienced overt acts of racism as an African-American assistant professor in a predominantly White institution. Racial slurs, prejudicial statements, and violence against another person based on race in public are not as acceptable today as they were in the recent past. Although overt racism may be coming back into 'fashion', such acts remain taboo in many professional spaces. Instead, I experienced covert racism and microaggressions. Covert racism is subtle, and hidden. It subconsciously works to harm, insult, and damage marginalized groups' psyches. This is the form of racism that makes you think you're mentally unstable because you cannot quite pinpoint racialized acts against your personhood, but you can *feel* them. You may ask yourself, "Am I imagining this or is this really happening?" I can recall several situations where I felt extremely uncomfortable in the classroom and questioned whether the discomfort was a result of student hostility, which stemmed from prejudicial views and/or racism, or my own imagination.

As an example, there was a time I was in a classroom with what I considered a hostile group of students. It was my second semester teaching full-time. I had made some changes to the lectures and assignments based on feedback I received the previous semester teaching the course. I spent considerable time and effort identifying, creating, and revising course materials and activities while the campus was in winter recess. This course had a lab component. I revised the lab assignments from observation reports to an observation portfolio. I thought that this change would allow space for students to select, reflect, and write about children's development that pertained to the observation experiences my students would have during lab. I provided written instructions for the observation portfolio assignment and a list of activities and observation prompts they could choose to focus on during lab. The observation portfolios would be collected at mid-term and at the end of the semester. Upon handing out this assignment, students repeatedly talked about being confused. They said they did not understand the assignment, and they did not know what was going on. To make the assignment clearer, I revised and reworked it. To keep up with students' demands for more and more clarity and information about the assignment, I was working early in the morning before my young children woke up and late at night after I put them to bed to make changes and still prepare for both of my courses. The more I attempted to revise the assignment, the more errors with dates and points I began to make. I knew that I was sinking, but I was not sure what to do about it. As I stood in front of the class explaining yet another set of adjustments to the assignment, a White female student shouted out, "You are unprofessional." I was mortified. I'd been called many things in my life, but never unprofessional. I could feel myself being choked by Frye's double bind. My heart started to pound, my mind began to race, and my ability to code-switch started to fade. My authentic code slowly overtook my facial expression and voice as I cocked my head to the side and said, "Excuse me?" There was a silence in the room, and I took that opportunity to regain my ability for the mainstream code. I calmly explained to her and the other students in the class that as the instructor, I was making changes to the assignment to meet students' needs.

The semester continued with the student who said I was unprofessional totally ignoring my instruction, searching the Internet while I lectured, and challenging all my feedback on her assignments. Adah Ward Randolph (2010) notes experiencing similar acts of disrespect as an African-American assistant professor:

> During class, I have been interrupted when talking to a group of students, interrupted when answering questions, disrespected by talking when I or other students were engaged in learning. They questioned when I informed them assignments were due. I experienced the shuffling of papers and the collecting of parcels before class was officially ended, and finally, I was called a liar by a student when asked about my personal experience to which she replied, 'BULL' in a very loud, antagonistic voice (p. 128).

We cannot make this stuff up. It is beyond my wildest imagination that I would become a professor, excited to educate the next generation of scholars, and be treated with such disdain by my students. The student who called me unprofessional was not the only person to behave in this manner in this class. There was a White male student who jumped in to *rescue* me, without an invitation, as I thought of an example of a concept I was discussing in class. On a separate occasion and later in the semester the same White male student laughed out loud during one of my lectures. In response to this second incident, I asked the student to refrain from such behavior as it was disruptive to the class. Two African-American male students in the class witnessed the act and found it necessary to speak with him about it after the class ended. At the end of the class, the White male student walked up and apologized to me. I accepted his apology. I also spoke with the African-American male students about my ability to hold my own and their need to maintain positive relationships with their peers.

There were several other events that took place with different students throughout the semester in this class that were blows to my humanity and dignity. I endured this for the entire semester. In hindsight, I realize I was dealing with the "dumb, Black, bitch stereotype" that is perpetuated in American society about African-American women. Historically, scientists conducted and published research on the intellectual inferiority of Africans and African-Americans to justify enslaving them in what is now the United States. Although the research has long been debunked, the stereotypes remains. To add, African-American women are often portrayed in the mass media as loud, disrespectful, angry, and rude, which creates additional stereotypes. According to Wingfield (2016), "the nature of these controlling images has potentially devastating consequences for minority men and women at work" (p. 432). In her research, Winfield identified Collins' (2004) modern Mammy and "educated, Black bitch" as interrelated and problematic controlling images African-American women encounter in the workplace that negatively impact their experiences. I now see that my first-year rookie mistakes as an assistant professor may have confirmed these stereotypes for some of the students in my class. As the modern Mammy, I was expected to bend to their desires and reinforce their senses of superiority; but I did not. Consequently, small groups of students created a hostile, racially charged environment in which I had to contend.

Although it was determined by a group of my peers and the Dean of the college that I was highly qualified during the hiring process, hostile groups of students openly challenged my competence, professionalism, and right to have the job. Consider the following quotes from the end of the semester student evaluation for this course:

> *Competence*: "The instructor does not prepare for class and oftentimes is not knowledgeable about class material. She is very rude and doesn't treat students

with respect"; "Unorganized: unclear expectations. Unprepared. Treated students like kids. Lack of depth of knowledge on topic. Seemed uninterested in teaching. Flustered easily"; "You did not know the information...."

Professionalism: "Gain a more professional approach to student opinions/constructive criticisms"; "I found the professor to be very unprofessional and disrespectful to students. The information was not presented well and when students asked questions they were disrespected in return"; "Unprofessional. Snide comments 'everyone else understands'...."; "More organized and professional with grading and assignments"; "Very unorganized, unprofessional, not ready to teach or open to constructive criticism"

Right to Have the Job: "The class was the worse I have ever taken. Find a new job!"; You did the worst job trying to give us the info in the book! Lectures were horrible and pointless. My grade is a joke cuz your ass! Worse class I've ever taken. You should be ashamed. . . Get a new job!"

I feel like I may be losing you, now. Some of you may be

thinking that I must have been a horrible teacher and that I am a despicable person, but, before you make up your mind about me, please consider the following positive comments from students who were in the same course at the same time:

Positive Comments: "She was very welcoming and seemed like she loved what she was teaching about"; "Wanted everybody to learn the material"; "I really enjoyed your class. It was well organized, and I like the fact that you took time to get the students' opinions about the class to help the class"; "Explains things well"; "Sometimes changed things but still does things <u>for</u> the students" (underline provided by student); "Very enthusiastic about the subject"; "Very helpful with instructions. PowerPoints very informational"

I was also teaching a second course that semester. It was my second time teaching this course as well. Although I received some feedback about organization, students' comments about my teaching and who I was as a person were positive:

Positive Comments from Second Course: "She was very kind and did her best to inform us about the info. Activities within the class made it fun"; "You're great keep it up!"; "You're great!"; "She made a great effort to clarify things and accommodate our learning. I appreciate that she asked for our input before the course ended. . .Keep up the great job!"; "Knows her stuff. Great attitude in class"; "Very organized details for assignments on BB"; "Try to be more clear of what you want of students, but, good job"; "Great job! Very energetic, happy personality made it a [joy] coming ☺ " (smiley face provided by student)

So, no. I am not a horrible teacher or a despicable person. But, I was dealing with constant hostility in the classroom and that hurt my performance. I felt threatened, and I was desperately trying to protect my personhood. Dr. Adah Ward Randolph noted in her autoethnographic account that among her students "25 percent will love me, 25 percent will hate me, and 50 percent will be in the middle" (p.124). I agree with her statement. Dr. Randolph also found that "it only takes a few" (p. 124) and "one student turned into an angry gang" (p.134). I also agree with this. In the course that I taught, I believe that the responses from the 25 percent of students who hated me had tipped the 50 percent of students in the middle toward their side of the scale by the end of the semester. Thus, creating a hostile and almost unbearable teaching environment.

Additionally, teaching was an embodied experience. So much so my physical health began to suffer. I developed a persistent cough and lost my voice for a few days. After being ill for a few weeks, I finally made time to see a physician. I was diagnosed with a sinus infection, which I had never had as an adult. After the sinus infection, my gums started bleeding and my mouth felt numb at different points during the day. I went to see a dentist and physician about these issues. The dentist did not find anything abnormal about my gums or teeth. The physician told me I had inflamed taste buds—what? I had never heard of it. I was also losing weight because I skipped meals to work. I was experiencing physical signs and symptoms of stress. In her autoethnographic account of her first few years as an assistant professor, Dr. Pauline Clardy (2010), noted:

> By year three, I had consistently worked hard and received excellent reports of my teaching even though I was dealing with a situation at home that required much of my time and energy—taking care of my elderly mother. I was determined not to allow my home responsibilities to interfere with my work at the university, and it never did. I paid nurses to attend to my mother while I worked, and I took care of her after work often without getting much sleep. The price that I paid is that at the end of each school year, I literally collapsed from exhaustion and ended up in a cardiac ward (p. 48).

Teaching was literally making me ill and weak. Dr. Maura Toro-Morn's (2010) reflection of her experiences teaching courses on race/ethnicity as a tenured professor in a predominately White institution after returning from sabbatical also exemplified the physical impact of teaching stress. She said, "Returning to teaching has been so hard and disruptive that it has made me physically ill. I woke up with a horrendous sore neck that sent me running to the masseuse" (p. 83). Teaching is something you experience, mind, body, and soul, which makes doing this work in hostile contexts mentally and physically debilitating.

I waited until the end of the summer to read the feedback from my courses. It was difficult reading those comments, and as I read them, tears streamed down my face. I relived the pain I felt in the classroom. A few of the students from that same course were enrolled in a course I was scheduled to teach for the first time in the Fall. I started to panic. I called my husband and cried out, "I'm not going back!" He told me that I was using the wrong matrices to evaluate my performance. He said I should not be concerned with what my students had written about me. But, *He* did not understand what *I* was going through. I felt like no one did. I was not getting any other feedback about my performance. The feedback from students was all that I had.

I decided to resign. I gave a semester's notice and made plans to finish out the semester with my department chair. It was extremely difficult. It turned out that I was right to panic about having students from the previous course enrolled in the one I was scheduled to teach in the following fall because the students from the previous course continued to show hostility. There was a point in my final semester teaching, after I had resigned, when I wanted to walk right out of the class. I imagined myself doing this as if I were outside of my own body watching it play out. But, I didn't. I held steady. But, I could feel myself shrinking back into myself, turning into a corner, and staying there as I played the final video clip of class, in the dark. I couldn't even look at my students. By the end of the class, I was shaking. Directly after class, I called my cousin and told her I didn't think I was going to make it through the rest of the final semester. She assured me that I could do it. Next, I called my husband and told him how I was feeling. He said that I should quit now. I should resign on the spot. Inside, I wanted to believe my cousin, that I could do it. After talking to my husband, I thought I had to resign or my inaction would signal that I was a glutton for punishment and didn't deserve his help or sympathy.

I decided to quit on the spot. I went directly to the department chair's office. I was hoping that she would not be in her office, but she was. I was hoping that she would not have time to see me, but she did. I told her that I would not be able to finish out the semester. I didn't want to be the reason why students were not learning. I started to cry. She offered me a tissue; I felt so pitiful. It was the second time I cried in front of one of my work colleagues that semester. I had never cried in front of people at work before. I was humiliated. She told me that she did not want me to have a bad experience my final semester. She said that they were learning something or else she would have heard from them; they would have come to her office and they had not. We talked about my feedback, and she offered to come to my class. She offered to release me from one or two of my classes. I realized that the section I had just left was the one that I felt the most hostility. I thought that she could take that one on. She asked if she could have two weeks to work on it. I said yes. She said that she wanted me to think about continuing so that I would know that I could do it. I said I would.

On the drive home, I regretted going to my department chair, because now she would think that I was a quitter— someone who could not be counted on, a bad worker. I cried again. I didn't feel like she really understood my plight. Later, at home, I decided to continue with all three courses and finish out the final semester as planned. At the end, I did it, and I was proud. I received negative feedback and evaluation from the section of the course I wanted to walk out. Ironically, for the other section of the exact same course that I taught my final semester, I received positive feedback from student evaluations. Again, a small group of students created a hostile, racially charged environment in which I had to contend with microaggressions twice a week for nearly 16 weeks. I am not able to articulate how truly difficult it was to be in those spaces. In the end, dealing with student hostility outweighed the positive aspects of my job. And, I was glad that I had left it.

Collecting My Thoughts on Experiencing Oppression as a Black Woman in Academia

I believe the negative comments I received for the courses with hostile students served to degrade and maintain the controlling images of Black women widely held in American society to objectify and thereby dominate this group. (Collins, 2008). Collins describes the controlling image of black mammy as "the faithful, obedient, servant" who despite having the ability to "wield considerable authority in her White 'family', the mammy still knows her 'place' as obedient servant" (p. 80). Students' notations regarding my lack of respect for them, is contrary to the controlling stereotype of mammy who accepts subordination from the White male and female power structure. By defying this controlling image, I became the "educated Black bitch." Bell hooks (2015) described the stereotypes of black womanhood within the U.S. historically to be dominated by images such this. For instance, she noted that the Sapphire conjured stereotypes of Black woman as "evil, treacherous, bitchy, stubborn, and hateful" (hooks, 2015, p.85). These caricatures of black women dominate the media. In two popular television dramas with African American female leads, the characters are esteemed professionals on the one hand and hypersexual and/or domineering women who become increasingly violent as the seasons progress on the other hand. The popularity of these programs suggest that these images of black womanhood are still pervasive in U.S. society. And with this as the cultural backdrop, I was racialized and oppressed in the classroom.

Microaggressions are subtle, they are brief, intentional and unintentional, occur in everyday life, and they hurt. Harris and Gonzalez (2012) argue that microaggression attempts to punish a woman of color who "acts like a serious intellectual rather than a mascot, cheerleader, or seductress" (p.3). In my case, microaggression played out in the form of constant questioning, posturing, inattention, and paternalistic feedback in which they chastised me and denigrated my performance because they could. My department chair said that students would be understanding of my position as a new professor who was learning along with them, but, many of them were not. Dr. Adah Ward Randolph (2010) recounted a conversation with a Black female student who said, "I could never be as calm as you are when students are being disrespectful. They never talk to the other professors in that way or question them the way they did you." Dr. Randolph went on to say that in one of her courses constant questioning became normal for her as a professor. "Oh, I am used to it. It was, in fact, the first day of class, and I knew I was in for 'one of those classes' where I am constantly questioned because I am African American and female" (p. 120). I was not able to "get used" to such treatment from my students.

As indicated by student feedback, I did not have any major issues or hostile students of note in the other course that I was teaching, and most of the hostility was felt in one or two classes. This just shows how covert racism and microaggressions, even when suggested by only a few students in one or two classes, can threaten your life. I was reading literature and receiving advice on how to cope with microaggressive acts of racism related to being Black in academia. Some suggestions were exercising, listening to music, giving myself a special treat, talking to other people, and seeing a therapist. I did not feel any of those suggestions would address the degradation I endured in the classroom and the impact it was having on my life. I wasn't really interested in coping. Why was the onus to succumb to insult and discomfort on the oppressed? Frye (1983) notes that:

It is often a requirement upon oppressed people that we smile and be cheerful. If we comply, we signal our docility and our acquiescence in our situation. We need not, then, be taken note of. We acquiesce in being made invisible, in our occupying no space. We participate in our own erasure. On the other hand, anything but the sunniest countenance exposes us to being perceived as mean, bitter, angry, or dangerous (p.11).

I wanted to resist it. I felt in my heart that there were people out there who could benefit from my skill set and appreciate my work. I told myself that I did not have to take it. So instead of coping with oppression as a Black woman in academia, I resisted the only way that I knew how and seemed feasible. I left.

3

BEING A MARRIED WOMAN WITH CHILDREN

"When family and work obligations collide, mothers remain much more likely than fathers to cut back or drop out of work. But unlike the situation in the 1960s, this is not because most people believe this is the preferable order of things. Rather, it is often a reasonable response to the fact that political and economic institutions lag way behind our personal ideals."

~Stephanie Coontz, *Why Gender Equality Stalled*, 2016, p. 363

Before getting married and having children, academic life consumed me. I was a graduate student, and I felt good about my work and where I thought I was headed—into a wonderful career of thinking, researching, and making a difference. I was so idealistic. I was also an officer in the Army Reserves, so I was working part-time. After passing my preliminary exam, I met an incredible person who was impressed by the fact that I was pursuing a Ph.D. and serving in the military. I was impressed that he was not intimidated by the fact that I was pursuing a Ph.D. and in the military. He had to relocate to another state for work shortly after we met, but we continued our relationship long distance. I made plans to join him after I completed my data collection, and before the big move, we decided to get married. After making the decision to move with my fiancé, I was offered a graduate assistantship. I wanted to take it because it was a wonderful opportunity to learn new skills that I wanted to add to my repertoire. But, I declined the offer because of my plans to relocate to the state my fiancé resided. This was the first work related action I took for the sake of family. Getting married and then later having children has had the most influence on my professional work life to date. Here are some other examples. I resigned my commission as an officer in the military after the birth of my first child to avoid the separation from my family that could occur as the result of a deployment. Then, I left my full-time job as a family life and human development specialist not long after my second child was born to have more flexibility to care for my children. Finally, I left my full-time job as an assistant professor because of the negative impact it was indirectly having on my family life.

My first job after completing my Ph.D. was as a family life and human development specialist at a university. It seemed like a perfect fit with my degree and interests in working in community settings. When I interviewed for the job, I was pregnant and due soon. I was not offered the job until months after my interview. Still, I was excited about the job and couldn't wait to get started. Although I knew I had to consider my husband's career options when evaluating the job opportunity, I didn't stop to consider what my needs as a new mother would be. So, I didn't ask about work hours, flexible work schedules, or child care options when the associate administrator called me on the phone and offered me the position. What it meant to be a working mother was not something that entered my mind in a substantial way. I always anticipated entering and staying in the paid labor market after I completed my degree, with or without children. It was a given since I had invested so much time and effort into pursuing an advanced degree. More importantly, I was not independently wealthy and came from a long line of women who had to work formally and informally to survive. Being an employed mother with children was something that I just planned to do—I thought it would all work out somehow. And it did work out for the first two months because my husband was job hunting and caring for our child when I started my new job. To add, my mother had come along with us for a couple of months to help us with our relocation. But, after my husband started his new job and my mother left town, I started to feel the pull of home. I was anxious about leaving my then 10-month old daughter in child care for 10 hours a day. I had to be at work from 8:00 a.m. (which I did not know until a week before starting the job) until 5:00 p.m. After an extensive search for high quality child care and switching providers a few times, I found a wonderful family daycare for my child. The one issue with this child care program was that it was closed one Friday a month. I began using paid leave to stay home with my child on the Fridays the child care program was closed. I enjoyed the time home with my child, so, initially I did not mind using paid time off. To add, I was fond of just about everyone in my office, and I was truly enjoying my work.

The adjustment to office culture was difficult, especially as a mother, but I made it work until I became pregnant with my second child. I was still new to the job, and I did not have much employee leave saved. The institution did not provide paid leave in preparation for or after the birth or adoption of a child; employees had to use sick and vacation leave for pay. I planned to be out the entire 12 weeks guaranteed under the Family Medical Leave Act (FLMA), so I had to do a lot of saving to have at least 30 days maternity leave with pay. This is when taking leave for a sick child or no child care, and the lack of a formal telecommuting policy at my place of employment became more problematic. I had not received any relocation funding for the job. Therefore, expenses and the loss of income associated with the move left my family financially vulnerable. I could not afford to be on maternity leave without pay. So, I started to advocate for myself. I advocated for telecommuting. It was denied. I advocated for a reduced appointment (¾ time). It was denied. So, I just kept on working and saving leave.

I created a plan to reduce my hours as I got closer to my due date because I realized I was going to have to work up to the day I went into labor if I did not. My supervisor was supportive, at the time, and she approved my plan to use my leave to gradually reduce my time in the office the month before my due date. My colleagues were wonderful! They generously donated leave to me while I was out giving birth to and caring for my second child. Because of their donations, I received my salary for almost the entire time I was on maternity leave. With help from my coworkers, I had made it work! However, after I returned to work from maternity leave, I found that my administration, at the department level, was much less supportive of my requests for workplace flexibility. The good news was I continued to do well at my job, and I began to hear about other job opportunities that might offer the flexibility I thought I needed to succeed in both roles— mother and worker. One job was as a tenure-track, assistant professor. I thought this was the answer to all the issues I was having being a working mother with young children.

My spouse was not excited about the assistant professor job at first because it required relocating again, but he told me to go and "win the job," and I did. He seemed caught off guard when I received my job offer, and he was resistant to the idea of moving for the position. I was confused. It seemed that he was proud of being married to a professional woman as long as her job opportunities didn't interfere with his career ambitions. He felt that I was jeopardizing his work situation by asking him to leave his job for mine—this would undermine his power and authority as a male in a patriarchal society. I was so disappointed. I didn't feel like he was supporting my efforts to balance work and our family obligations. He also told me that he didn't want to move because he was happy where we were. But, what he did not seem to realize was that he was only happy with our situation because I assumed most of the extra child care and housekeeping duties while he traveled for work. I was the one running around the city transporting children from place to place and nursing them back to health from illnesses. I was also fighting for flexibility at my job; something he already had as a sales engineer. He was happy in his patriarchal bubble, and I was exhausted. For the first time, I saw my spouse as someone who was oblivious to my reality as a woman. He seemed consumed by what bell hooks (2001) described as "the black male quest for recognition of his 'manhood'" (p. 100).

I was determined to take advantage of this opportunity to become a tenure-track professor despite my spouse's protests about relocating. I thought it would help the entire family. After a lot of negotiating that involved pointing out win-wins and agreeing to a commuter family situation that allowed him to stay at this job, my spouse was on board with relocating for my assistant professor position. I also promised him unlimited flexibility and exciting summers filled with traveling and good times. Well. It didn't quite turn out that way, but who knew?

Before receiving my teaching assignment for my new job as an assistant professor, I received an email from the department chair asking if I was okay with teaching a course at night or if I needed to switch it out due to child care constraints. One of my new colleagues, thoughtfully and proactively, considered this as a potential need and wanted to get my feedback. I wasn't sure what to say. On the one hand, I didn't want my new colleagues to think that I was not a team player or that being a woman with children would get in the way of doing my fair share of work. On the other hand, during my campus visit, I recall telling everyone who would listen about my desire for a flexible environment that worked well for my family. Furthermore, my spouse planned to travel for work, and I was not sure what I would do for child care yet. So, I decided to tell my chair that I did not prefer to teach the course scheduled in the evening. Everything worked out, but, I began to sense that my assistant professor position was not going to be as flexible as I thought it would be.

As an assistant professor, I was still primarily responsible for caring for the children and household. For the first year, my spouse spent a lot of time traveling for work, which meant I was solo parenting most of the time. At one point, my husband was only home on the weekends. He was really disturbed by being what he called "a weekend dad," and I was worn out from working around the clock, even on weekends, to keep up with the demands of my new job and being our children's primary caregiver.

I called a mentor to talk about how I was beginning to think that my new job was not a good fit for the lifestyle I wanted. She encouraged me to keep trying, to find additional help, and she shared stories about how other women with young children she knew successfully navigated the tenure process. She said something like, "I know you want to stay home and bake cookies, but you need to ask yourself why you want to do that." She was right. I did want to bake cookies with my children. I did want to prepare healthy meals for them each day, and I did want to spend quality time with them in the afternoons and on the weekends. Why was the pull to perform these activities so strong? Why couldn't I seem to work and do these things as well? I thought about the women I knew who worked full-time and did all these things at home and I began to wonder, "am I weak?" Why was it so easy for my spouse to be content with our children being in child care for extended periods of time, and it wasn't for me?

I listened to my mentor's words, and I was encouraged to stay for the moment. I tried to find additional child care help, but it was not always easy. The stress was taking a toll on my entire family. When I tried to discuss what I was going through with my husband he would say, "You can quit." For a year, each time he said you can quit, I went down to my office and worked as hard as I possibly could because I did not want to quit. While driving home from a family outing one day in the summer, I began to feel the stress of the new semester. I had an article that I had taken along to read because that's how I had to live my life—maximizing every moment to get work done. I was on edge and my husband said he knew why. He pointed out the fact that I had my article with me. Again, he said, "You can quit." He only wanted me to be happy. I said, "Okay." And just like that I accepted defeat. Instantly, I felt relief.

The night before I formally resigned my assistant professor position, I called one of my mentors on the phone to discuss my decision. My mentor said that being a mom and working as an assistant professor was hard, and she understood why I wanted to leave. But, I did not leave my job because it was hard; I enjoy hard work. Although this was a convenient answer, I could not bring myself to say that I was leaving my job only because I wanted to take care of my children either. I felt like saying that would do women everywhere a disservice. As a married woman with children, I left the workplace because the cost associated with having it all was too high; it required doing it all. When faced with what I believed to be a choice between being the best worker that I could be and being the best mother that I could be, I believed then and still do, that I would be happiest being the best mother that I could be. But, this belief did not jive well with my feminist ideology. Even though I believed that I would be happier at home with my family, leaving my professional job as an assistant professor to engage in motherwork on a full-time basis, also meant that I had ascribed to a traditional gender role expectation and given up a part of myself. I felt ashamed, empowered, and upset all at once. I felt ashamed that I had fallen prey to gender role norms and socialization. I felt empowered by my ability to stand up for myself and say no, I will not work two shifts; it's one or the other. And I was extremely upset that I was entangled within the double binds that characterize systematic oppression that were making being a married woman with children difficult to navigate full-time employment.

Collecting My Thoughts on Experiencing Oppression as a Married Woman with Children

Second wave feminism provided strong rhetoric that women can do anything men can do. This is true in theory but, remains elusive in practice. Gender equality has yet to be realized in the United States. Women have access to fewer resources in comparison to men and face more obstacles by being women. The notion that women and men are the same minimizes the strengths and undermines women's unique needs and qualities in various situations. As a woman, my need to physically give birth to a child, something a man has never done, was unique. Although we were both becoming first-time parents, my husband and I did not have the same needs. My spouse seemed fine, but, I needed more options to successfully integrate work and family obligations within the current social structure and economic system.

A Facebook friend asked in a post, #canwereallyhaveitall, #skeptical. My response was, "Good question. Structural inequalities still work to oppress women in our society; so, I don't think so, #tradeoffs." My Facebook friend's response to my post alluded to the fact that she didn't think gender oppression was the reason that she could not have it all as a telecommuting mother of two whose husband traveled often for work. She suggested that it was a family issue not a women's issue. Coontz (2016), author of the article "Why Gender Equality Stalled," noted the following:

Our goal should be to develop work-life policies that enable people to put their gender values into practice. So, let's stop arguing about the hard choices women make and help more women and men avoid such hard choices. To do that, we must stop seeing work-family policy as a women's issue and start seeing it as a human rights issue that affects parents, children, partners, singles, and elders (p. 364).

Yes, I believe the lack of national work-family policy is clearly a human rights issue, but, I also believe that it is through the oppression of women that this human rights violation operates. Therefore, it is a women's issue. Although it is difficult to recognize our own oppression as women because we will simultaneously have to come to terms with the role we play in perpetuating it, we must acknowledge gender oppression to bring about social change.

I left both of my jobs because gender oppression still exists; society's expectations of women do not match our realities. Social norms and gender socialization still privilege men's experiences over women's and result in institutionalized inequality. Social structures have not changed enough to support women's full participation in the workforce after having children. More specifically, job sharing, paid maternity leave, and part-time work opportunities with full benefits do not exist universally and are hard to come by in the U.S. That is part of the reason why I left the workforce.

4

BEING A FULL-TIME WORKER

"In a society where the good is defined in terms of profit rather than in terms of human need, there must always be some group of people who, through systematized oppression, can be made to feel surplus, to occupy the place of dehumanized inferior."

~Audre Lorde, *Sister Outsider*, 1984/2007, p. 114

Although I was only in the paid labor market for five years as a full-time worker before leaving, I started working for pay at the age of 14. My first job was helping a neighbor with housekeeping a few days a week. In addition to other part-time jobs and appointments, I was also in the Army Reserves for 13 years before starting my first full-time job. During the time I was in the paid labor force full-time, I found myself advocating for my rights as a worker.

Working an Eight-to-Five as a Woman with Children

As mentioned before, my first job out of my Ph.D. program was as a family life and human development specialist. I was extremely excited to get the verbal job offer and salary for this position. However, the hiring manager later came back with a salary that was $5,000 less than the initial offer. Even though I was new to salary negotiations, I was confident that an initial salary offer should not go down during the process. My level of excitement started to wane as I grappled with the lower salary offer along with knowing that I would not receive relocation assistance if I decided to accept the job. Instead of paying me what my work was worth and providing the relocation funding that I needed to avoid financial hardship, I would be hired as cheap labor because I "did not have experience." I talked with some people that I trusted about the offer. They gave good advice, but they seemed to think that turning down the offer was an option for me to take. However, I had been on the market for almost a year, and I was beginning to feel desperate. Before even starting the job, I was in a double bind as a worker. I could either decline the offer and continue my job search in a limited market or accept the lower salary offer and go into debt to relocate for the job. I settled upon going into debt with the lower salary offer.

Upon accepting the job, I encountered other hidden issues. According to one of my new colleagues, I was required to report to work from 8:00 a.m. to 5:00 p.m. I thought that the nature of my work would afford me some flexibility with this schedule, but I soon learned that flexibility was limited. I was expected to be in the office from eight to five, Monday through Friday, unless I was on work-related travel. Transitioning into this mode of work was difficult. Working in the office and adhering to an eight to five schedule presented ideological challenges. As a graduate student, I had complete control over where and when I worked. Although I kept a detailed personal schedule to manage my time and activities, this was not required. So, I essentially had more work flexibility as a graduate student than I now had after earning a doctoral degree and I did not understand why. Nevertheless, I had accepted the job and relocated, so I had to figure out how to be a worker and a mother with an infant in this environment. To adhere to the eight-to-five schedule, I had to drop my daughter off at daycare at 7:30 a.m. at the latest, and the earliest I could pick her up was 5:30 p.m. By the time we arrived home in the evening, I had about 30 minutes to interact with my child before starting dinner. My spouse took care of her while I cooked, or he cooked if he did not have to travel for work. We had dinner around 7:00 p.m. and then got ready for bed by

7:45 p.m. Out of 24 hours, I only spent about 3 hours a day with my child while she was awake. I constantly felt pressed for time as I rushed around trying to pick up, drop off, and complete tasks by a certain time.

A couple of months into my new job, I realized that the eight-to-five schedule was going to be problematic for me because we had to navigate two demanding full-time jobs as a dual earner family. So, I began advocating for flexible work arrangements. I asked for an earlier start time so that I could spend more of my child's waking hours with her. My supervisor at the time approved my request to change my schedule. I started arriving earlier, at 7:30 a.m., so that I would have more time to interact with my child in the evening and to cook dinner on the days my spouse traveled. Though I was still stressed about time, I typically left professional work at the office and relaxed and enjoyed time with my family on the weekends. However, normal events like illnesses and travel became major problems to solve in our household because we were busy professionals. Additionally, we lived over 700 miles away from our extended family members who may have been able to provide some support when we needed it. To manage duties at home and work, I requested the option to telecommute a couple of days a week from my department level administration. The response I received was that I could work from home on occasion for specific purposes but not on a consistent basis or in a formal capacity. Again, I had difficulty understanding why I was being denied what I needed to be a successful worker. The work that I was performing could be completed from any location with Internet and a phone connection.

I knew this because I had colleagues at our sister institution, in the same position, who had been enjoying an organizational culture where flexible work hours and telecommuting was the norm. What was going on? Why did my administration want control of my body? Was it because as a Black woman worker I needed to be surveilled under the watchful gaze of others to do my job? Well, the rationale my leadership provided against flexible work hours and telecommuting at the institution I worked with was: prior 'abuse' of workplace flexibility by some employees in the past. This explanation was not enough to deter my interest in telecommuting because as a new employee I did not see the value of being penalized for behaviors of other employees that took place before I was even employed there. Furthermore, I felt like strong leadership along with organizational culture and policies that motivated employees to do their best work would address issues of productivity better than denying telecommuting altogether because of employee abuse. Sandberg (2013) notes that:

Technology is also changing the emphasis on strict office

hours since so much work can be conducted online. While few companies can provide as much flexibility as Google or Facebook, other industries are starting to move in a similar direction. Still, the traditional practice of judging employees by face time rather than results unfortunately persists. Because of this, many employees focus on hours clocked in the office rather than on achieving their goals as efficiently as possible. A shift to focusing more on results would benefit individuals and make companies more efficient and competitive (p. 131).

Despite my thoughts about the organizational culture, I continued to follow my institution's expectation of working in the office. However, I advocated for myself as a worker as much as possible in the process, and it was tiring.

After returning from maternity leave to care for my second-born child, I met with my new supervisor and one of the items we discussed were work hours. I asked if I could resume my 7:30 a.m. to 4:30 p.m. schedule, which I had negotiated with my previous supervisor, and she said no. She said that I would have to come in from eight to five "like everyone else." At this point, I had been a very successful professional. I won a major grant; I was writing an academic paper; and I was performing all the work associated with my job well, as far as I knew. In fact, before taking maternity leave, the administrator told me that this same supervisor complimented my work ethic. When I brought this compliment up to my supervisor to strengthen my case for flexibility, she said something along the lines of, "Well that's when you only had one child." I was in shock. Nothing about my work ethic had changed because I had two children. But, for some reason, the administration did not think I would be able to perform my job if I was given more flexibility.

This struggle that I was having at work was all happening amid backlash against telecommuting which was created when the new executive president of Yahoo! ended the practice at that organization. I was fired up about workers' rights and the need for institutions to respond to the changing lifestyles of the workforce. To add, my spouse was traveling more than ever for his job, and I was now caring for two small children alone two to three work days per week. I tried to organize other women at my job to collectively protest rigid workplace policies. Once, one other specialist was willing to talk to our supervisor together about the need for flexibility. I did not know that I was engaging in institutional activism. I just wanted change; but, nothing changed. I continued to struggle.

One morning, I decided I was going to stand up for my rights as a worker and make one last attempt to change the workplace environment so that it was more flexible. I asked to telecommute one Friday a month. My request was denied, and

I slid my two-week notice of resignation across my supervisor's desk. It was a bold move, which my leadership team did not expect. The day after I resigned, I was told innocently by a colleague that a different institution would not have even hired me without experience. My intuition was telling me that her point was that I should stop complaining and be happy that I was given the job, especially since I didn't have any "experience." I could not just be happy to have a job, because I am not a machine. I am a human being with needs, wants, and desires other than just having a job. Now it was a matter of principle, and I was more than prepared to stand behind my decision to resign, but I didn't have to. The dean of the college received my resignation letter and asked for a meeting. The dean said he was willing to allow me to telecommute one Friday a month to meet my child care needs, so I rescinded my resignation.

I thought this would be a win for the entire office. Many of my colleagues also disliked the lack of workplace flexibility. However, instead of becoming a heroine at work, I became an outcast. I think some people in leadership may have felt like I went behind their backs to get what I wanted, but I did not. I asked them in a very direct manner, even in writing, for what I needed to make the job fit with my family obligations several times before resigning, and they would not bend. I had even been told that organizations do not change for individuals,

individuals change for organizations. I was not able to change for the organization; my family needed me. I also felt like a couple of coworkers did not feel that they could be associated with me after I rescinded my resignation because I was now seen as "the trouble-maker." They did not want to become outcasts as well. They let me know that they couldn't just quit their jobs like I did. They needed their jobs. And I understood. At the same time, I felt that as a worker, I had to do what was best for my family. The double-bind was ever present. No matter what decision I made, I lost something. I continued to work in this emotionally charged state until I was offered an opportunity to work as an assistant professor. Even though my new position did not start for several months, I gave my second notice of resignation right after signing my new job offer.

Overworked Mother in Academia

As I transitioned into my role as an assistant professor, work began to feel much more familiar. I had a general idea of what was expected of me in terms of productivity and had freedom in how I met those expectations. I also had some flexibility in terms of where I completed my work and when. However, as a self-proclaimed overachiever, having unlimited work hours was problematic. I ended up working constantly. Because I was new to the job, there was a steep learning curve that I had to navigate. As I mentioned in chapter two, there were several tasks I had to work on at once, such as prepping and teaching two new courses. It was explained to me that course prep and teaching were expected to take place simultaneously. Although I had negotiated one course release in both the Fall and Spring semesters, and I was teaching two courses instead of three, and despite having started preparing the courses in the summer, my course preparations were still largely incomplete when the Fall semester began. I had the syllabi prepared and textbook and readings identified, but I still had to create presentations, develop assignments, evaluate students' performances, teach twice each week and hold office hours for two different courses. I also participated in departmental meetings, acclimated to the campus, and did motherwork. This workload was unrealistic, and I think that my first year as an assistant professor was a complete disaster because of it.

I was overworked. I rose early in the morning to work from home before waking my children and getting them ready for the day. I worked in my office after dropping them both off at their different early childhood programs, before class meetings. I worked at home again in the afternoon after picking up my oldest child from her early childhood program that ended at 3:30 p.m., until I had to pick my youngest child up from daycare and start our evening routine. I even worked late at night after I put my children to bed and finished household chores. On the weekends, when my spouse was typically home and took care of the children, I worked some more. I was essentially working all day long, almost all the time. This was odd because I was working more hours and making less salary than I was in my previous position. I was not being paid for all the work that I was doing.

What was most disconcerting about my new life as a faculty worker, was the normalcy of all this work in the context of academia. I started to feel perturbed when people would ask, "How was your weekend?" I would reply that I spent it working, and I would receive a knowing nod. I wanted them to be bothered by the fact that I was working on the weekend. I was bothered because weekends were supposed to be family time. I also started to become uncomfortable with responses to my statements of how much I was working with, "You know the first year is difficult, it's all about survival," as if it had to be this way. I would think, well if the first year is this difficult for everyone and this is common knowledge, maybe something should be done to change this. Or when I said, "I wish I had more time to prep" and the response seemed to be there was no time to be given. I would think, "Why not?" Is it a funding issue, or a personnel issue? What is the barrier to giving new professors time to prepare to teach before they start teaching? In the middle of my struggle with my daily work life, there were endless debates going on regarding tenure standards. Some people seemed to be arguing for more rigorous standards of productivity. I recall sitting through one of these discussions and thinking that I could not possibly do more work than I was doing in that moment and saying to myself, "These people must want me dead. I have to get out of here!" And I know that having tenure brings workers a sense of comfort and security, but I started to question whether I wanted the guarantee of having this job and lifestyle forever. It really didn't seem all that attractive to me anymore because I began to equate tenure with constant work, or feeling guilty about not working. Once, I was in a meeting and there was a discussion going on about workload, and I accidentally said out loud, "How much work are we supposed to be doing?" After a response was made, I quietly asked, mostly under my breathe, "What about quality of life?" I could feel the double binds....

Not only was I working all the time, but, my hard work did not seem to be paying off. As noted in chapter two, students were highly critical of my performance. I believe that racism played a significant role in some students' criticisms, but I also believe that not having time to fully prepare my courses before teaching them exacerbated the impact of the covert and microaggressive acts of racism that unfolded throughout the semester. I was still prepping the class and mastering the content as the semester went along. I made a lot of mistakes. It was like a domino effect. The more I worked, the less I slept. The less I slept, the more mistakes I made. The more mistakes I made, the more microaggression I experienced in the classroom from disgruntled students. The more I experienced microaggressive acts of racism, the more I wanted to leave the job.

I think having the paid work time I needed to prepare during my first year would have made a difference in my ability to cope with the demands of my new job. Instead, I started losing my confidence and becoming increasingly alienated from my work. I had left my previous position as a family life and human development specialist feeling like a confident and successful professional who had been able to hold her own with the best. Now, I was just trying to survive, and I was barely keeping my head above water. A former department chair once shared a story of one of her assistant professors having a nervous breakdown her first year on the job. This story began to periodically creep into my mind during my first year as an assistant professor, and I would feel overwhelmed, but I determined that I would not have a nervous breakdown; I had two children who were depending on me. As the image of having a nervous breakdown loomed overhead, I knew I had to survive mentally intact. At the end of my first year, I was proud of myself for surviving. But, I was battered and bruised due to systematic oppression I experienced as a Black woman worker in academia.

To add fuel to the fire, I was scheduled to teach a new course in the fall of my second year. Although a senior faculty member warned against taking on too many new course preps, I felt a need to replace one of the courses from my first year with a course more closely aligned with my research area. So, I added a new course prep. Now, I had two new course preps going into my second year. As the new semester approached, I started to become nervous because although I spent much of the summer working (unpaid again) to prepare to teach the new course, it still was not fully prepped. At the beginning of August, I transitioned my children from part-time child care to full-time so that I could work longer hours to get as much done as possible. In the car, the day my spouse noticed that I had work materials with me, on a family outing as described in the previous chapter, I had a few moments to take a step back, and I realized that work had begun to totally take over my life. Almost suddenly, I realized I was not going to able to fulfill the promise of exciting summers filled with travel that I made to my family when I left my family life and human development specialist job to become an assistant professor. I was always working and because of the move, we did not have extra money (relocation was not available for the assistant professor position either).

Even with the job change, my lifestyle was still not what I

knew it could be and wanted it to be. Ward and Wolf-Wendel (2012) described academia as a 'greedy institution' where the ideal worker works all the time. In both of my positions, I experienced, though unstated, high workplace demands for my time, energy, and loyalty. I voluntarily complied with these institutional expectations and had given them power over the way I lived my life (Egger De Campo, 2013) for five years. My job as an academic was not fulfilling my needs at a critical developmental moment in my life. I decided that the power I willingly gave these institutions over my life was no longer legitimate. I decided that life was too short to allow work to monopolize all my time, so I decided to leave, yet again.

Collecting My Thoughts on Experiencing Oppression as a Full-Time Worker

Black women have always had to work and often under the watchful gaze of the White established order and as unpaid laborers. Black women's status as workers is embedded in a history of economic exploitation as they were "disenfranchised within the US political economy" (Collins, 2008, p. 55). After leaving my jobs, women at both institutions talked about how they wished they could quit too, but they were the primary earners for their families. I realize that being able to leave a job without ending up homeless or hungry is a privilege in our current economic system not many people, particularly Black women, can access. I am troubled by the fact that many women must work jobs that do not allow them to adequately fulfill the other roles in their lives because their entire families are depending on their earnings to survive.

As a worker, I was in two situations where I felt I had to stand up against oppression. It was challenging because I was young and considered inexperienced in both contexts. As a new employee, particularly in academia, some of the advice I received was: don't say anything; go with the flow so that you don't seem disagreeable; and just observe. I tried, but to no avail. Instead, I asked for what I wanted and felt I needed. I spoke up about policies and practices that I thought would adversely impact me as a worker, and I left when my needs were not met. I guess I never cared about making waves or appearing disagreeable—after all, this was the part of my temperament that enabled me to achieve so many of the accomplishments that I had by the age of 35.

One of the things that still stands out to me in my efforts to advocate for myself as a worker is that I knew that I was not alone in how I felt about the workplace because people would discuss feeling similarly. However, what Karl Marx described as a "class consciousness" never emerged. Instead, people were afraid to speak out. I understood that, but it was still a hard pill to swallow because as a 'lone ranger' I was easily dismissed and labeled as a troublemaker by those in leadership. I felt alone, and it was hard doing this work by myself. I also was afraid, which is why I did not say half of the things that I was thinking, most of the time. I would have liked to have said: (1) in our current society telecommuting is not something to run away from, it should be embraced and leaders should be given strategies to better manage it; (2) the tenure process needs to be revamped; (3) new professors should be allowed time to prep courses before teaching them for the benefit of themselves as professionals and most importantly the students that they serve; and (4) just surviving in your job is unacceptable and should not be the norm; instead, being set up for success in tangible ways backed by financial resources should be a given for workers. Unfortunately, I was too afraid to say any of those things in public. However, I am not afraid anymore. I know that silence will not help the people who are in these situations recognize their oppression and become free.

I don't think people see the oppression women face in the workplace today. Nevertheless, the fact that women may appear weak or inadequate when asking for workplace accommodations, or they may almost kill themselves working around the clock if they do not ask for accommodations represents a double bind. Both outcomes have negative consequences. It may seem like women are making individual choices about work and family, but, social institutions, expectations, and sanctions determine what women are able to do when it comes to work and family. Women, such as myself, still predominately major in subjects and work in fields that continue to be undervalued and underpaid. As a woman with a Ph.D. in social science, I made less than my male spouse with a BS in engineering. He made almost double my salary; this made my jobs more likely sacrificed for the sake of the family than his jobs. Sexism made my exit from the paid labor force the better financial option for our dual earner family in this capitalist economy.

To add, work is not always liberating for women. I have come to realize that in many ways, my professional work was indeed oppressive. According to bell hooks (2015):

Contemporary women's movement was extremely class bound, as a group, white participants did not denounce capitalism. They chose to define liberation using the terms of white capitalist patriarchy, equating liberation with gaining economic status and money power. Like all good capitalists, they proclaimed work as the key to liberation. . . Implicit in the assertion that work was the key to women's liberation was a refusal to acknowledge the reality that, for the masses of American working class women, working for pay neither liberated them from sexist oppression nor allowed them to gain any measure of economic independence (p. 145).

Hooks stated, "Feminism has been used as a psychological tool to make women think that work that they might otherwise see as boring, tedious, and time consuming as liberating" (p.105). Leaving both of my jobs were political acts because I turned my back on the expectation from the work world that I should be content in an unhappy work environment just to have a job. I was able to free myself from worker oppression in the paid labor market.

I left two different jobs. Twice, I did as many African-American women did after the institution of slavery was abolished in the U.S. who decided to "donate their time to home and children" (Jones, 2010, p.49). Does that make me an accomplice to my own gender oppression? Or does it make me an activist committed to gaining access to liberating work? I think this makes me an oppressed worker in another double bind.

5

MOVING INTO FULL-TIME MOTHERWORK AND PART-TIME EVERYTHING ELSE

"A less developed but equally important theme concerns how Black women's unpaid family labor is simultaneously confining and empowering for Black women. . . Scholarship suggests that Black women see the unpaid work that they do for their families more as a form of resistance to oppression than as a form of exploitation by men."

~Patricia Hill Collins, *Black Feminist Thought: Knowledge, Consciousness, and the Politics of Empowerment*, 2008, p. 52

I grew weary from fighting for my rights in the workplace (Jones, 2010) and at the end of the day, I just wanted to go home and not return. Anne-Marie Slaughter wrote an article, "Why Women Still Can't Have It All," for the Atlantic magazine that was published in the summer of 2012 about leaving a prestigious position in government to have more time to devote to caring for her family. In this thought-provoking article she noted:

> One of the most complicated and surprising parts of my journey out of Washington was coming to grips with what I really wanted. I had opportunities to stay on, and I could have tried to work out an arrangement allowing me to spend more time at home. I might have been able to get my family to join me in Washington for a year; I might have been able to get classified technology installed at my house the way Jim Steinberg did; I might have been able to commute only four days a week instead of five. (While this last change would have still left me very little time at home, given the intensity of my job, it might have made the job doable for another year or two). But I realized that I didn't just need to go home. Deep down, I wanted to go home. I wanted to be able to spend time with my children in the last few years that they are likely to live at home, crucial years for their development into responsible, productive, happy, and caring adults. But also irreplaceable years for me to enjoy the simple pleasures of parenting. . .

I wanted to go home and be with the people I loved and who loved me. I wanted time with my family and to experience life, with all its trials and tribulations, in a loving and supportive space. I did not want to fight anymore. I was tired. Giving myself permission to leave was the best gift I have ever given myself. However, life has not been without ups and downs.

Being Lost/Experiencing Loss Due to Leaving

My last day of paid work was December 31, 2015. After this day my health, mood, and general disposition seemed to shift in a new direction. The first thing I did was crash. I stopped all professional work. I could not seem to get enough rest. However, the initial relief I felt after making the decision to leave and submitting final grades did not last long. I spent the next several months crying and questioning all my decisions to include having pursued a Ph.D. in the first place. These feelings were more about leaving academia than taking on motherwork full-time. I felt lost without my job. I wrote the following in my journal on July 6, 2016:

> *I did not sleep well last night. I kept thinking about my life and where I will go next. I do not have any definite goals. For so long, I thought that having an academic position would be where I ended up. But now, I feel lost.*

I thought my time had been wasted and having a Ph.D. was now worthless. In Jacqueline Jones's (2010) book, she provided an example of an African American mother's response to her daughter's decision to stay home full-time:

Frances Luckett, a school principal in Maryland, expressed reservations about her well-educated daughter's decision to stay home with her children full time. 'A lot of financial sacrifice went into helping her get two degrees,' Luckett added, 'There are no guarantees in life, and I worry that if she just gives up her career, is just a wife and a mother, she will have nothing to fall back on" (p. 287).

I shared this mother's reservations after leaving my paid employment for full-time motherwork. In my mind, there was a linear path for how my life would unfold when I enrolled in graduate school in 2002. I would complete my Ph.D., start a family, and become a professional. My life has not taken that linear path; there have been lots of bumps and twists in the road. Due to my temperament and the deviations I've made, including leaving my jobs, at times I felt that I had given up my career and I had "nothing to fall back on."

I also felt an incredible sense of loss regarding my income. In changing my status from being employed full-time in the paid labor market to doing unpaid motherwork, I had to come to terms with no longer being able to financially provide for my family. I took a huge financial loss and temporarily (if not permanently) diminished my earning power. Not only am I still paying costs associated with job relocations that did not fit with my family life, I lost salary, benefits, and retirement funding since leaving paid full-time employment. I am the poorest I've been since leaving home for college at the age of 18. This is ironic because I worked so hard to receive the highest professional degree in my field to escape the poverty that I endured as a child, and now I have little to no money associated with my name. I lost my financial independence.

I also lost my professional status and leaving my jobs may impede future pursuits to reenter the paid labor market full-time. I have already found updating my LinkedIn profile and resume challenging. After entering an end date for my assistant professor position, the system kept prompting me to enter my new position information, and I did not have any to add. I was finally able to update my LinkedIn profile with my part-time job information after a while. Having a gap in my work history may cause potential employees to question my professional dedication and worth as a worker in the future. I have applied for part-time positions and received the infamous question, "Why did you leave your previous position?" I realize that an acceptable answer to this question does not exist. I will always get this question in interviews and notes of the "gaps" in my employment history will be taken when potential employers and colleagues review my CV or resume. People that I know have shown concern over my decision to leave. They would ask, "Where are you going?" I would say, "home," and they would have puzzled looks on their faces. People tried to convince me to stay after I gave notice of resignation to my university. They were not shy about saying that they thought as a professional, I would regret leaving paid, full-time employment. I have found that motherwork is not considered a professional occupation by many people that I have encountered.

(II)Legitimizing Black Women's Motherwork

I experienced unexpected push back regarding leaving paid, full-time employment for full-time motherwork. After I left my job as an assistant professor, several people offered unsolicited advice on how I could find another job. I also get questions like, "What are you doing now?" from former colleagues and relatives. For example, during a family outing with my children and some other relatives, my (un)employment became the topic of discussion. Here is the journal entry from June 26, 2016:

I had breakfast with [relatives] and the subject of my (un)employment came up. He asked me what I was doing (in terms of work) now. I said "nothing." I don't think this was a good enough answer for him because he went on to ask if I would be teaching online. I told him probably not since I had not heard back from the university I applied to. He asked if I wanted to teach; I said a little bit, but, not a lot.

Then, he asked a philosophical question and said something like, look, let's be real. You went through a lot of school to get your degree; don't you want to give back to society? [My children] were sitting on either side of me in their chairs, and I stretched out my arms behind them and said, "I am contributing to society." In reflecting on this incident, I wonder why people think pursuits within families are less valuable than those of the workplace? Sad. My [relative] went on to give ideas of what I could do to give back (he obviously was not convinced that I was doing enough by taking care of my children). Then, he finally offered, "you can go back to school, you're good at that." I replied, "I have worked! I had two jobs." I told him that I want my work to fit within my family life; not for my family life to fit within my work. I realize that I am doing a lot of work. It is not recognized, nor valued, nor paid.

Just under a year later, the same relative asked my spouse something like, "Why can't [J. Kelly] get a job?"

I even challenged the worth of my motherwork. I constantly felt the need to do something in addition to taking care of my family, and I have yet to focus solely on motherwork. In fact, soon after I left my assistant professor position, I finished a couple of writing projects I was working on. I applied for jobs, but only those that fit the lifestyle I want to have. I wrote a grant. I started writing a business plan. I applied for and took on part-time paid employment, and I completed a few scholarly projects, including writing this book. I have not determined whether I was motivated to do these things by my desire to maintain my status as a professional or the financial obligation I felt to help my family make ends meet. It was probably a combination of both.

Nearly two years after leaving my assistant professor position, I am slowly coming to understand and legitimize my motherwork. I am embracing motherwork, and I have found that it is mentally and physically draining. I function at elevated levels from the time I wake up and start my morning routine until I wind down in the evening. Since taking on full-time motherwork, I complete most household and caregiving tasks for my family. It is hard work. I took time to create a working list of jobs that I have, or I am performing for free that would be paid if someone in the labor force was performing them for my family:

- Before and Aftercare Provider
- Part-Time Preschool Teacher
- Reading Coach
- Domestic Worker
- Robotics Coach
- Capital Developer

- Accountant
- Event Planner
- Driver
- Nurser-of-Children-Back-to-Health
- Summer Camp Director and Leader

Writing this list helped me name and legitimize the motherwork that I do and assign value to it. I should have earned a conservative estimate of $30,000 for reproductive work, household labor, and community development activities that I performed last year, but I was not paid. In addition to these, I started out trying to do almost all the child care and household tasks while my spouse worked outside of the home. However, I soon realized that although I was engaged in motherwork full-time, there were still too many household and caregiving tasks for me to complete alone, so my spouse and I had to readjust our expectations and renegotiate the workload. Because of renegotiating, my spouse has taken on more responsibility for housekeeping and child care. He has altered his work schedule (he had a much less challenging time doing this than I did) to incorporate tasks like dropping off and/or picking our children up from school, preparing dinner here and there, and supervising our children's bedtime routine. He does this work in addition to various budgeting (shared), maintenance, and home repair tasks. Even though my spouse actively participates in reproductive labor, I am still the primary caregiver and caretaker of our children and household.

The good news is, although I am juggling several household jobs, I've created space to redefine myself as a scholar. I do intellectual work on a part-time basis. I also engage in volunteer work as a board member for two nonprofits and with the local school district. At first, I thought that my efforts to establish myself as a scholar were wasted since I was no longer employed in the paid workforce. Now, I am envisioning myself as an intellectual outside of the confines of traditional employment. While interacting with Black feminist thought, I now understand that "the concept of intellectual must itself be deconstructed. Not all intellectuals are educated. Not all Black women intellectuals work in academia" (Collins, 2008, p. 18). Although I would like to be paid for my motherwork, I have become content with working for my family full-time and everything else part time. On August 5, 2016 I wrote, *"Quitting my job has awakened a sleeping giant. How free I feel to speak! Less preoccupation with the job has meant more time for deep reflection and meaningful exchanges."* Over the years, I had fallen into the capitalist trap that privileges profit over all else. Being able to finally realize working for institutions for pay did not offer more, but less freedom and independence, was a breakthrough. I am currently redefining myself and the work that I do. Although my career had not taken the linear path that I naively thought it would, I'm at a place where I feel more at ease. Leaving was an act of resistance and taking on motherwork full-time has been liberating. Tired of fighting and neglecting my family, I walked away from it all and slowly embraced the freedom to reimagine myself and my work. Still, I do not enjoy being economically vulnerable as a result.

Collecting My Thoughts on Experiencing Oppression as an Unpaid Motherworker

Patricia Hill Collins (2016) contends that economic provision has long been integrated into African-American women's definitions of motherhood; with roots in West African tradition and in response to racial and gender oppression in America. Because I see myself as a Black feminist, and I ascribe to this Afrocentric motherhood ideology, leaving the workforce has been difficult. It has required that I face painful contradictions. I want to enjoy motherwork, but because it is unpaid, undervalued, and low status, I am forced to become aware of the ways in which I am participating in my own oppression. Double binds are evident and although there may seem to be a way to escape, as an individual Black woman worker, there is not. Even though I was able to free myself from an oppressive labor market, I remain in a double bind. So, there is still pain.

I am working to understand why engaging in full-time motherwork seemed illegitimate to people that I encountered. Is it because I am a Black woman, and Black women are always expected to work under the surveillance of and in service to the public instead of their families? According to Jones (2010):

As 'free' laborers, the former slaves should be bound not

by the institution of bondage but by labor contracts negotiated annually with a landlord. In to this view, Black women 'worked' only when they labored under the watchful eye of a White person in a field, or in a kitchen, but not when they cared for their own families at home (p. 44).

Is it because I have a Ph.D. and I am expected to use it in conventional ways (after all, I using my degree in human development and family studies daily in my private life) in the labor force? Is it that I am a woman, and progressive women are expected to work outside of the home in service of the public, and earn money independently?

Historically, Black women who attempted to regulate their labor outside of the home were considered lazy due to racist ideologies and controlling images of the time. These racist ideologies still exist today. In fact, the myth of the 'welfare mother' may be at play in my current situation. Covington-Ward (2013) said, the "Welfare Mother is another negative stereotype, emerging post-World War II and explicitly connecting ideas about Black women's fertility to state assistance programs" (p. 250). People may be questioning me about "staying home" because the thought of me working only for my family conjures negative images of single, Black women sitting at home all day providing inadequate care to many children and receiving tax payers' money that they do not deserve. The contribution that African-American women, across social class subgroups, make to society through child rearing is negated by the controlling image of the welfare mother. This controlling image serves to undermine Black women's motherwork. I think that as a Black woman, I may not appear worthy of full-time motherwork to some people. Even I doubted the legitimacy of my own motherwork initially.

In the process of interrogating my thoughts about motherwork in the context of controlling images of African-American women, I have been able to move past those doubts. I know that the work that I perform for my family and community is valuable and worthwhile. Jacqueline Jones (2010) noted that during and soon after the Civil War, "Black women demonstrated that they would seek to put the interests of their families first" (p. 44). Like these women, I proudly labor on "my own terms and attend to [my] own household." Like my female ancestors who were able to leave the labor market in the past, I have done so:

Not to mimic middle-class White women's domesticity but, rather, to strengthen the political and economic position of their families. Their actions can be seen as a sustained effort to remove themselves from the exploited labor force in order to return the value of their labor to their families (Collins, 2008, p. 61).

Leaving paid professional employment was an act of love, resistance, and commitment to an ideal that I have for my life. I decided that the lifestyle that I wanted for my family was more important than the economic value my work had outside of the home. Although my thoughts about motherwork have changed, societal views and controlling images remain the same.

Before reflecting on my experiences leaving paid, professional work, I thought that I was quite progressive. Now, I see that in theory I was, but in practice I was not. There are some pitfalls of full-time motherwork. For instance, gendered divisions of labor are more pronounced, sharply delineated, and traditional (male provider, female caretaker) in my family now that I am home full-time. On the other hand, when we were a dual-earner family and I worked from eight to five, my spouse and I shared the housework. During this time, we even paid for housekeeping services to free both of us up on the weekend to spend time together as a family. However, we soon realized that we could not afford housekeeping services coupled with our child care expenses, so we only had these housekeeping services intermittently. And, although I happily outsourced household tasks as a dual earner, I was more reluctant to relinquish the care of my children to people outside of my family for extended periods of time. Though there were a couple of times when I was working full-time and my spouse was in-between jobs (for periods of 4-8 weeks) that he provided full-time care for our children and the household, I have been the primary caregiver since my children were born.

My family's participation in the workforce, in combination with our gender socialization, contributed to the reproduction of traditional gender roles within my family. In many of the books I read about women successfully navigating work and family, the need was stressed to have a partner or spouse who was willing to share household responsibilities or take them on full-time (e.g., Ward & Wolf-Wendel, 2012). My spouse and I were both willing to share household and child care responsibilities; however, structural and ideological roadblocks were in place that we didn't realize were impacting our family life. In the current political economy, when all parents work in a household, they are susceptible to overwork, fatigue, and stress unless they are financially able and emotionally willing to outsource reproductive work. However, when women (or men) engage in full-time reproductive work outside of the labor force, they are unpaid. Unpaid work can lead to financial hardship for families who are one generation removed from poverty, such as mine, or are working poor, and therein lies a double bind.

Woman's reproductive and household labor are vital work that must be carried out for society to function. Evidence of this are the jobs that must be outsourced when all available parents are in the labor force full-time. However, work outside of the family continues to be worth more than work within the family in this capitalist economy. Not only that, but when men are paid more than women for the work they perform in the labor force, work that men do tend to take priority over and seem more important than work that women do. Traditional divisions of labor are perpetuated by worker oppression and the devaluation of the work people perform for families and communities within and outside of the paid labor force.

Black women workers are simultaneously acting in the context of racial oppression, which means they are not given permission or encouragement to drop out of the oppressive labor force. Black women who do not work in the paid labor force often experience the negative controlling image of the undeserving "welfare mother." I was asked to explain why I wasn't working and my plans to re-enter the labor force on several occasions. I felt that I was expected to work no matter the impact working had on my well-being and/or family life. I rejected this expectation first unconsciously, and then directly. After the initial grief of leaving my job, I interrogated larger social issues impacting my personal troubles. I found that Black women workers, paid and unpaid, are in lose-lose situations despite individual effort and perceptions of choice. Black women historically have been unable to control their labor because their bodies were stolen and held hostage by sexist and racist oppression. As I reflect on what my foremothers endured as workers, I shed silent tears. They suffered injustice, humiliation, disrespect, and the burden of caring for other people's families at the expense of caring for their own in the same ways. I am extremely grateful to these women and their abilities to exist in matrices of domination and still love their daughters enough to say, you do not have to endure what I endured. These women were my mother and others' mothers, and they endured so that I would not have to suffer in the ways that they suffered. I could leave. I could resist. And, I could go on. And I did. And I am. Motherworker.

6

CONCLUDING THOUGHTS

"The caged bird sings with a fearful trill, of things unknown, but longed for still. . . For the caged bird sings of freedom."

~Maya Angelou, *The Complete Collected Poems of Maya Angelou*, 1994, p. 195

So, there you have it. I left full-time, paid, professional work because I was unhappy, and I wanted to change that. I also left because I could leave; I had resources available to me that made leaving a viable option. I now realize that the reason it was hard to answer the "why did you leave" question when asked was because it was personal and complicated. It was not just being **Black** or being a married **woman** with children, or being a **worker** that negatively impacted my experiences in the labor market. It was the embodiment of all those experiences as they intersected within the larger political economy and socio-historical context—I was discontent with it all. I was operating within multiple systems of oppression that required me to constantly navigate double binds. As a Black woman worker, it became painfully clear that I would always be scrutinized and heavily penalized for real and imagined mistakes I made in the workplace, particularly the classroom, and for speaking out and up for myself as a worker and woman with children. There was no singular event that pushed me out of paid, full-time employment, it was everything all at once.

In the workforce, my choices were limited. They never adequately addressed the issues that I was having without creating new issues to address. In the moment, they seemed to be private challenges that I should solve alone or with my spouse. Upon hindsight and critical reflection, I realize I was caught between systematically related structural barriers that limited my ability to exist outside of the system and freely choose courses of action without penalty. I was like Frye's caged bird. Leaving paid, full-time employment was not a free, individual choice for me because it was made within systems of oppression (related to racism, sexism, and worker exploitation). I employed all of my 'super powers' to survive as a married Black woman with children in the workforce, but, they were no match for the various forms of oppression that I was up against.

The penalty for leaving was quite high—personally, professionally, and financially. I lost my personal assets, professional status, and financial resources in the process of leaving the workforce. I did not receive esteem or reward for standing up against oppression in the workplace, instead I was questioned, labeled, and left traumatized. Now, I am a full-time motherworker. And, even as a person in a professional identity crisis, with no real income, limited employment options, and working for little to no pay, I am happier. I still resist oppression while engaged in motherwork. But, the motherwork that I do does not injure my psyche, so my resistance feels different. I enjoy laboring on my own terms and with the people I love.

Recently, I was asked to teach a graduate course online, and I agreed. I hope the time that I have taken to reflect on my experiences in academia will be beneficial when I go back into the trenches. Honestly, I do not know what will happen beyond that in terms of paid employment. I'm still soul searching. I will continue to seek out opportunities to use my talents, and I am excited about my future.

Notions of Help or Support

In the introduction, I talked about C. Wright Mills's concept of the sociological imagination. Throughout my story,

I shared my personal troubles, while identifying public issues that I thought contributed to them. I have concluded that workplaces as institutions operate in ways that perpetuate racist and sexist oppression for Black women workers, and they are inflexible and greedy. I would be remiss if I did not draw upon my sociological imagination to offer some solutions to these public issues. Frye (1983) argues that within systems of oppression false "helpfulness" is often given while "real" help is denied. In the same way, I was offered help as a Black woman worker that was not always helpful or practical. I was given advice such as: work more; get help with your children; get your spouse to do more work at home; write grants, ignore the student evaluations; and hold on, it will get easier. These suggestions, though well-intentioned, were not helpful because they did not address the larger structural issues that I and many other women of color workers face. With Frye's quote in mind, the following reflects what I think would have provided the real help I needed to cope with my personal troubles and that might help address larger social issues causing them.

End Racist and Sexist Institutional Culture

While in the paid workforce, I felt as if my personhood was constantly under attack, and I had to fight off assaults each time I stepped into the doors of my workplaces. This was especially true in my experiences in academia (for certain courses). I experienced extreme battle fatigue fighting the presumption of my incompetence.

Personally, I could have helped myself by doing more research on institutions I worked for before accepting the job offers. Regarding my job as a family life and human development specialist, I should have found out about salaries, work schedules, travel demands, and resources (Clardy, 2010) before I accepted the job offer and I could have declined the offer to work in a place where the policies perpetuate sexist oppression. I should have also researched the university I joined as an assistant professor more. I tried to get a feel for the university during my campus visit, but staying a few additional days and visiting class meetings of faculty of color may have provided a more accurate understanding of the racial climate. Actions that I took as a Black woman worker that were beneficial and offered real help in workplace were making reasonable requests for flexibility and leaving inflexible and hostile environments. For Black women workers in situations whereby double binds require that you stay in hostile workplace situations despite racism and sexism, as bell hooks (1989) suggests, create communities of resistance to sustain yourselves and combat matrices of oppression. Having a safe space or being associated with a community of resistance may have been helpful in my situations.

The onus is not only on individuals; organizations must

provide real help to Black women workers. It would have been helpful to have financial resources and time provided by the institution for me to engage in self-care work (therapy, exercise, relaxation, etc.) that research suggests faculty of color who struggle being oppressed and resisting oppression in the academy need. Fighting injustice is arduous work that Black women workers take on, not because we want to but because we must to survive with our personhood intact. In the short term, we should be paid more for working in emotionally hazardous, racist, and/or sexist environments.

A sustainable and long-term solution to change the racist and sexist organizational culture of the workplace is to create an atmosphere where being socially just is the norm. All new employees and incoming students (if in a university setting) should receive training on how oppression and white supremacy operate in society and are reproduced in the workplace. In academia where new faculty are subject to constant surveillance by administrators, more senior faculty, and students, there should be zero tolerance for demeaning behavior towards them, period. Black women workers should be particularly safeguarded due to historical and contemporary experiences with controlling images like the mammy, sapphire, and educated Black bitch. In academia, faculty and administrators should not depend solely on student evaluations to determine faculty teaching effectiveness, and they should create campus environments where social justice is valued in theory and practice. Wilson (2012) provides a good list of additional forms of real help that I think will begin to redress institutional cultures of sexism and racism. I quote from page 77 of her chapter:

1. conduct cultural audits to assess the 'temperature' of the climates in their academic units

2. administrators accept responsibility for cultivating a supportive and inclusive climate

3. academic administrators and leaders must demonstrate that all faculty are valuable and competent members of the campus community

4. examine [your] own knowledge regarding women faculty of color and the challenges they face

5. demonstrate a commitment to cultural competency

6. provide resources so that women can attend conferences and/or join professional organizations

7. conduct exit interviews with departing faculty to determine the reason they are leaving institutions and consult with faculty who have remained to identify factors that can aid retention.

Although these recommendations focus on academia, I think they can be applied to U.S. workplaces in general.

To end racist and sexist institutional culture, we must name sexism and racism within the larger society. By remaining silent, we communicate that everything is working to our satisfaction. Sandberg (2013) noted:

> Staying quiet and fitting in may have been all the first generation of women who entered corporate America could do; in some cases, it might still be the safest path. But, this strategy is not paying off for women as a group. Instead, we need to speak out, identify the barriers that are holding women back, and find solutions (p.147).

Ending racism and sexism is everyone's work. I hope that people who read this book will be empowered to name and challenge sexism and racism in public spaces by "talking back" and standing up for others to end and dismantle oppressive policies and practices in favor of a more progressive anti-racist and anti-sexist society.

Redesign Inflexible Institutions

Great Places to Work is a think tank that collects feedback from individuals employed at different organizations on workplace culture using surveys. According to their report, "The Best Workplaces for Flexibility," companies with flexible arrangements such as telecommuting, job sharing, compressed schedules, flex time, and culture that supports flexible arrangements are great places to work. In my first job as a family life and human development specialist, I was searching for this kind of flexibility and organizational culture, but it did not exist. Not only was workplace flexibility nonexistent, telecommuting seemed to be something to prohibit and tightly control. Even though there was no formal policy, I requested flexible time, a compressed schedule, and a 30-hour work week at reduced pay. Any one of these options would have been helpful to me as a worker, but none were available.

The existence of the FMLA as it stands as a federal workplace policy is only minimally helpful. I took advantage of the Family Medical Leave Act after I had my second child. The leave was not paid. In Canada, the Employment Insurance (EI) program offers new parents temporary financial assistance. The EI program provides up to 35 weeks off for parents to share. Also, "A maximum of 15 weeks of EI maternity benefits is available. The 15 weeks can start as early as eight weeks before the expected date of birth, and can end as late as 17 weeks after the actual date of birth" (Employment Insurance Maternity Paternity Benefits, 2017). In the U.S., unpaid leave is guaranteed for only 12 weeks, which does not begin until after you give birth. What a difference! According to Boushey and Williams (2012), "the United States is the only country among the top 30 industrialized democracies in the world that lacks paid maternity leave" (p. 103).

When it comes to issues of flexibility, some institutions should redesign workplaces to offer real help to women in the paid labor force and their families. As, Sandberg (2013) stated:

Too often rigid work schedules, lack of paid family leave, and expensive or undependable child care derails women's best efforts. Governmental and company policies such as paid personal time off, affordable high-quality child care, and flexible work practices would serve families and society well (p. 102).

Although, some organizations are doing this, many are not. Efforts to bring about change should be large scale and at the national level. This would include workplace legislation. Coontz (2016), author of "Why Gender Equality Stalled," noted:

Astonishingly, despite the increased workload of families, and even though 70 percent of American children now live in households where every adult in the home is employed, in the past 20 years the United States has not passed any major federal initiative to help workers accommodate their family and work demands (p. 362).

We need legislation that supports work life integration for all women and their families to improve the situations of Black women working.

Federal legislation lags behind our social needs. However, there seems to be some discussion related to addressing this neglect at the federal level. A subcommittee hearing, 'Balancing Work and Family: What policies Best Support American Families,' took place in 2007 and holds promise. But, the questions I still have are why aren't these conversations part of a national discussion, how long will these conversations continue to take place, and will they lead to change? To create the national changes needed to truly help women and families, workers will have to develop group consciousness, demand change from our legislators, and then make change happen together.

Place Limits on Greedy Institutions

Dismantling structural barriers by decreasing the number of hours workers are expected to contribute in the workplace. As an academic, I had the 'freedom' to work 60 to 70-hour work weeks. I soon realized that I was not at all free. Most of my waking hours were dedicated to work; to the detriment of my family life, physical health, and emotional wellness. I would have benefited from real help in the form of workload reduction. I did receive help from a long-time mentor with negotiating my academic job offer that included two course releases the first year in the job; I taught two courses each semester of my first year. This might sound like a light teaching load, but it was not in the context of the 'invisible' work that I was responsible for as well.

Real help would involve changing the greedy culture and ideal worker norms that guide workers behaviors and expectations. This could be done by ending the culture of overwork, allowing and supporting professional workers in adhering to reasonable work hours (in the case of academics adhering to the nine-month calendar their salaries are based on), and making invisible work (writing letters of recommendations, informal mentoring, late night meetings, etc.) more visible. This is particularly important for new professionals who also need time to do all the invisible work of getting to know organizational culture, and trying different approaches to doing their jobs.

The importance of mentors and mentorship programs is well documented. Mentorship can be important for some people (Clardy, 2010). But, Black women workers need more than mentorship to be successful in the workplace. Although it helps to know the rules of the game, mentorship does not help change the rules to make them equitable. I found that mentorship fell short of providing the real help I needed to succeed in the workplace. Playing by faulty rules helps reproduce institutional inequality. An apprenticeship or coaching model may offer more real help to new employees.

New professional development models in the field of teacher education use coaching to assist novice teachers in the classroom. I suggest academia and similar organizations institutionalize onboarding policies that allow employees a full year of preparation and apprenticeship (watching, learning, and doing) prior to expecting them to execute job-related tasks independently.

Work can also be scaffolded to ensure employees do not experience overwork after starting a new job or taking on a new role. I met a person who taught only one graduate level course, related to her dissertation research, her first year as an assistant professor. Then, she was expected to teach a different course the following year. This seems helpful because the person could begin her teaching career from a place of strength. She had depth of knowledge and possibly years of experience with the content area gained from writing a dissertation that she could draw from to teach during her first year in academia. Then, additional courses would be gradually scaffolded onto her existing experiences. I think this is real help and is counter to the sink or swim approach to onboarding that workers experience in the workforce. Being set up for a successful transition is especially important for Black women workers who operate in the context of the controlling images described throughout my story. Black women workers require safe spaces and opportunities to begin their professional careers from a place of strength because of heightened visibility, presumed incompetence, and their marginalized status in the workplace.

Legislation for a national 30-hour work week is what we need today, along with living wages, to limit greedy institutions from taking control of our lives and to help individuals integrate work and life. Only collective action will result in the systemic changes we need to dismantle the structural impediments to self-actualization for all workers and their families in the U.S and abroad.

Recognize the Value of Motherwork

Bell hook's (2015) notion of parasitic relationships described in *Ain't I a Woman*, suggests that women benefit from patriarchy and participate in their own oppression when they leave the workforce and/or engage in motherwork full-time while their male spouses work in the paid labor force full-time. I think this notion devalues woman's unpaid reproductive labor—vital work that must be carried out in society. The ideology that motherwork contributes less to a family system than earning money perpetuates sexist oppression in the matrix of domination. While many people tried to be 'helpful' by giving me tips on how to do less at home and more in the workforce, the real help I needed was a shift in paradigms of thought around caring for others. This would lead to greater value associated with motherwork. Everyone loses when paid employment drives our actions to the extent that the work of caring for others is an afterthought. Women engaged in motherwork are not parasites; they are performing critically important work by caring for families and communities.

It is true, as a full-time motherworker, I am dependent upon my male spouse and his employers for food, clothing, and shelter. Motherwork is mentally challenging, physically exhausting, and emotionally rewarding; however, there are little to no financial incentives for those of us doing this work full-time for our own families. Motherwork, like many of the jobs held predominately by women in a patriarchal society, is undervalued. Society should reward women engaged in motherwork on a more commensurate manner to include increased prestige, paid time away from the workforce to care for families and communities, tax incentives, national health care, and access to the highest quality universal child care opportunities, just to name a few. Also, providing wages directly to individuals (men or women) who labor for others in their home and communities would offer the real help to people like myself whose reproductive labor and civic engagement support the workforce.

Final Words

In telling my story, I've made the personal public to

uncover and problematize being a Black Woman Working. This was not an easy task because I am left completely exposed. Based on some of the concerned looks on people's faces when I shared my plans to write an autoethnography of my experience leaving paid employment, I may have put myself at risk for something bad to happen—I'm not sure what else could possibly go wrong though. But, such is life, and so be it. This work is for the next generation of Black, Women, Workers, including my daughters, who will enter these spaces. This work, though it put me at risk, was a "labor of love".

I am grateful that I recognized that something in my life was amiss—that I was not fulfilling my promise and purpose. Freeing myself from my mental "cage" and naming my oppression has allowed me to exist in new spaces that are ripe with opportunities. Because of many women before me, I had the courage to write my story and even publish it. I am not hiding inside of myself any more. I am confronting the ghosts, Angela Mae Kupenda (2012) described at the end of her essay "Facing Down the Spooks." I was encouraged by her statement:

> I think the ghosts will fade when—instead of becoming speechless—we identify them for what they are. The more we give voice to a reality that suppresses these illusions, the closer we will move to being able to function together in the real world. No, the spooks are not behind the door!

They are present and dwell in our lives and structures and institutions, in a society that pretends that racism, sexism, and all the other -isms do not exist. Just remember: what we face down cannot harm us (p.27).

I've been afraid of so much for so long. I am not afraid anymore. I know that silence will not help the people who are in the positions I was in as a worker, and I want to help them. I am also grateful that I had the courage to walk away from something that I thought meant so much to me, professional employment, so that I could rediscover self and what I want to do with the rest of my life. I am reinvigorated by my desire to be a change-agent and cultural activist working to educate, uplift, and bring others along. Collins (2009) notes that:

Prevailing definitions of political activism and resistance misunderstand the meaning of these concepts for Black women's lives. Social science research typically focuses on public, official, visible activity even though unofficial, private, and seemingly invisible spheres of social life and organization may be equally important (p. 217).

I rearticulated participation in activism as a Black woman in the context of my everyday life and experiences in true third-wave feminist form. Black women have rarely had the privilege nor have been "content with merely nurturing their families and communities because the welfare of those families and communities is profoundly affected by injustices that characterize U.S. political, economic, and social institutions" (Collins, 2008, p. 222).

Jones noted (2010) "for the foreseeable future, at least, the resourcefulness of black wives and mothers would continue to represent that particular combination of love and sorrow that had for so long endured at home and on the job" (p. 298). As Black women workers, we must each find our "own way, recognizing that [our] personal biography, while unique, is never as unique as [we think]" and work collectively in "rejecting the dimension of knowledge that perpetuates objectification, commodification, and exploitation" (Collins, 2008, p. 308). I have found that one person cannot fight systems of oppression alone. Together, we must use the powers we have at our disposal to formulate solutions to the issues we face as Black women workers. We must to do more than talk about it. As the saying goes: we need to be about it. This should not be difficult because history shows that we've been about it. Angela Davis (1983) wrote:

This was one of the greatest ironies of the slave system, for in subjecting women to the most ruthless exploitation conceivable, exploitation which knew no sex distinctions, the groundwork was created not only for Black women to assert their equality through their social relations, but, also to express it through their acts of resistance (p. 23).

In our collective struggle, we can start dismantling systems of oppression that are roadblocks to the happy existence we desire, deserve, and can achieve. Although we may be trapped by double binds we must still "sing of freedom".

REFERENCES

Angelou, M. (1994). The complete collected poems of Maya
    Angelou. New York, NY: Random House.

Balancing work and family: What policies best support American
    families? Hearing before the Subcommittee on
    Workforce Protections, Committee on Education and
    Labor. House of Representatives, 110th Cong. 1 (2008).

Boushey, H. & Williams, J.C. (2012). Programs
    supporting working families will boost the economy. In
    M. Young (Ed.), Opposing viewpoints: Work and family
    (pp. 97-103). Farmington Hills, MI: Greenhaven Press.

Clardy, P. (2010) Amazing grace: Examining one
    woman's induction in the academy. In C. Cole Robinson
    & P. Clardy (Eds.), Tedious journeys: Autoethnography
    by women of color in academe (pp. 35-59). New York,
    NY: Peter Lang Publishing, Inc.

Collins, P.H. (2016). The meaning of motherhood in
    Black culture and Black mother-daughter relationships.
    In M.B. Zinn, P. Hondagneu-Sotelo, M.A. Messner, &
    A.M. Denissen (Eds.), Gender through the prism of
    difference (5th ed.), (pp. 361-364). New York, NY:
    Oxford University Press.

Collins, P.H. (2000). Black feminist thought: Knowledge, politics
    and the consciousness of empowerment (1st ed.). New

York, NY: Routledge.

Coontz, S. (2016). Why gender equality stalled. In M.B. Zinn, P. Hondagneu-Sotelo, M.A. Messner, & A.M. Denissen (Eds.), Gender through the prism of difference (5th ed.), (pp. 361-364). New York, NY: Oxford University Press.

Covington-Ward, Y. (2013). Fighting phantoms: Mammy, matriarch and other ghosts haunting Black mothers in the academy. In S. Nzinga-Johnson (Ed.), Laboring positions: Black women, mothering and the academy (pp. 236-256). Bradford, ON: Demeter Press.

Davis, A.Y. (1983). Women, race & class. New York, NY: Vintage Books.

DeGruy, J. (2005). Post traumatic slave syndrome: America's legacy of enduring injury and healing. Portland, OR: Joy DeGruy Publications Inc.

Duffy, M. (2007). Doing the dirty work: Gender, race, and reproductive labor in historical perspective. Gender & Society, 21, 313-336.

Eggers De Campo, M. (2013). Contemporary greedy institutions: An essay on Lewis Coser's concept in the era of 'hive mind'. Czech Sociological Review, 49, 969-987.

Employee Insurance maternal and paternal benefits. (2017). Retrieved from:

https://www.canada.ca/en/employment-social-
development/programs/ei/ei-list/reports/maternity-
parental.html#h2.1-h3.1

Frye, M. (1983). Politics of reality: Essays in Feminist Theory.
Berkley, CA: Crossing Press.

Great Places to Work. Best workplaces for flexibility.
Retrieved from
https://www.greatplacetowork.com/resources/reports/
632-the-best-workplaces-for-flexibility

Harris, A.P. & González, C.G. (2012). Introduction. In
G. Gutiérrez y Muhs, Y. Folres Niemann, C.G.
González, & A. P. Harris (Eds.), Presumed incompetent:
The intersections of race and class for women in
academia (pp. 1-14). Boulder, CO: The University Press
of Colorado.

hooks, b. (2015). Ain't I a woman: Black women and feminism
(2nd ed.). New York, NY: Routledge.

hooks, b. (1989). Talking back: Thinking feminist, thinking
Black. New York, NY: South End Press.

Jones, J. (2010). Labor of love, labor of sorrow: Black women,
work, and the family, from slavery to the present. New
York, NY: Basic Books.

Kupenda, A.M. (2012). Facing down the spooks.
Introduction. In G. Gutiérrez y Muhs, Y. Folres

Niemann, C.G. González, & A. P. Harris (Eds.),
Presumed incompetent: The intersections of race and
class for women in academia (pp. 20-28). Boulder, CO:
The University Press of Colorado.

Lorde, A. (2007). Sister outsider: Essays and Speeches. New
York, NY: Ten Speed Press.

Mills, C.W. (1959). Sociological imagination. New York:
Oxford University Press.

Muncey, T. (2010). Creating autoethnographies. London:
SAGE Publications.

Pew Research Center. (2015). The whys and hows of
generations research. Retrieved from http://people-
press.org/2015/09/03/the-whys-hows-of-generations-
research

Sandberg, S. (2013). Lean in: Women, work, and the will to
lead. New York, NY: Alfred A. Knopf.

Slaughter, A. (2012). Why women still can't have it all. The
Atlantic. Retrieved from
https://www.theatlantic.com/magazine/archive/2012/
07/why-women-still-cant-have-it-all/309020

Toro-Morn, M.I. (2010). Migrations through academia:
Reflections of tenured Latina professor. In C. Cole
Robinson & P. Clardy (Eds.), Tedious journeys:
Autoethnography by women of color in academe (pp.
35-59). New York, NY: Peter Lang Publishing, Inc.

Ward, K. & Wolf-Wendel, L. (2012). Academic motherhood: How faculty manage work and family. New Brunswick, NJ: Rutgers University Press.

Ward Randolph, A.L. (2010). What does racism look like? An autoethnographical examination of the culture of racism in higher education. In C. Cole Robinson & P. Clardy (Eds.), Tedious journeys: Autoethnography by women of color in academe (pp. 119-148). New York, NY: Peter Lang Publishing, Inc.

Wilson, S. (2012). They forgot mammy had a brain. In G. Gutiérrez y Muhs, Y. Folres Niemann, C.G. González, & A. P. Harris (Eds.), Presumed incompetent: The intersections of race and class for women in academia (pp. 65-). Boulder, CO: The University Press of Colorado.

Wingfield, A. H. (2016). The modern mammy and the angry Black man: African American professionals' experiences with gendered racism in the workplace. In M.B. Zinn, P. Hondagneu-Sotelo, M.A. Messner, & A.M. Denissen (Eds.), Gender through the prism of difference (5th ed.), (pp. 361-364). New York, NY: Oxford University Press.